How to Benefit from the Divine Liturgy

METROPOLITAN YOUSSEF

Edited and translated by
St. Mary and St. Moses Abbey

How to Benefit from the Divine Liturgy
By Metropolitan Youssef

Copyright © 2025 Coptic Orthodox Diocese of the Southern U.S.A.

All rights reserved.

Designed & Published by:
St. Mary & St. Moses Abbey Press
101 S Vista Dr, Sandia, TX 78383
stmabbeypress.com

All Scripture quotations in the footnotes of this book, unless otherwise indicated, are taken from the New King James Version® Copyright © 1982 by Thomas Nelson, Inc. Used by permission. All rights reserved.

The following Septuagint text is used when indicated: *The Septuagint Version of the Old Testament*. (London, UK: Samuel Bagster and Sons, 1879).

Contents

Introduction ... 5

CHAPTER ONE
Two Aspects of the Fellowship in the Divine Liturgy ... 8

CHAPTER TWO
How to Achieve Fellowship in the Divine Liturgy ... 17

CHAPTER THREE
A Brief Explanation of the Structure of the Liturgy ... 31

CHAPTER FOUR
How to Prepare Myself for the Divine Liturgy ... 35

CHAPTER FIVE
In the Divine Liturgy, I Understand… ... 44

APPENDIX
Four Fellowship-related Words ... 69

Introduction

One of the main features or characteristics of the ministry of Pope Kyrillos VI was the Divine Liturgy; he was a man of prayer, particularly of the Divine Liturgy. He prayed the Divine Liturgy every day, and he was committed to attending Midnight Praises and to praying the Offering of Evening Incense every day. I remember in the first memorial of His Holiness Pope Kyrillos VI, Pope Shenouda said, "I do not think that there is anybody in our contemporary time who has prayed as many Liturgies as Pope Kyrillos VI." With all the responsibilities as a patriarch, I wonder how he was able to commit to praying the Divine Liturgy every single day. But what does this mean? It means that, besides being a man of prayer, he enjoyed and loved the Divine Liturgy; otherwise, why would he commit himself to such a commitment, which appears to be impractical to me, as a clergyman, to commit yourself to praying the Liturgy every day. The reason why he was committed to this was that he definitely benefited from the Divine Liturgy, and he definitely found joy in celebrating it every day. That is why I would like to reflect on how to benefit from the Divine Liturgy—how to enjoy it.

Fellowship in the Divine Liturgy

When we meet together around the Altar of God and pray, at the end of the service, we take Communion. As we read in the Holy Scriptures, the Lord said, "Unless you eat the flesh of the Son of Man and drink His blood, you have no life in you. Whoever eats My flesh and drinks My blood has eternal life, and I will raise him up at the last day. For My flesh is food indeed, and My blood is drink indeed. He who eats My flesh and drinks My blood abides in Me, and I in him.... He who feeds on Me will live because of Me."[1] As the Lord said, this is the real body of our Lord Jesus Christ, and this is His real blood. And through the power of the Holy Spirit, the Holy Spirit changes the bread and wine into the Body and Blood.

Why did He give us His body and His blood? Because we are mortal beings, but His body is life-giving flesh, so His body gives life. When we are united with His body, then on the last day, we will be raised and will live for eternity with God.

When we meet together in order to pray, and at the end of the prayer and worship, we partake of His body and His blood, this prayer is called Liturgy. The

---

1   John 6:53–57.

word liturgy comes from a Greek word meaning "the work of the people." So, why do we call this "liturgy"? Because one person by himself cannot celebrate it. I cannot come by myself and celebrate the Liturgy. A communion of people, a fellowship of people, has to meet, gathered together around the table of God, around the table of the Lord, and we pray. The Lord said, "For where two or three are gathered together in My name, I am there in the midst of them."[2] In the Liturgy, there is a fulfilment of this promise.

When we come together, and pray and worship together, then God is among us on the Altar. And if you think about it, there is no greater work or activity than the Liturgy. Can you tell me about any activity you do in which you will have Christ with His body and His blood physically with us on the Altar? None. So the Liturgy is the greatest activity that we, the believers, do because in this Liturgy we have Jesus Christ, Emmanuel our God, physically with us on the Altar, by His body and His blood. Not only that, but He gives us His body and His blood, to feed on Him and to live forever.

---

[2] Matthew 18:20.

1

Two Aspects of the Fellowship in the Divine Liturgy

The Liturgy is the communal service, the work of the people. That is why one person alone cannot pray the Liturgy. The priest by himself cannot pray the Liturgy. One priest and one deacon cannot pray the Liturgy. To have a Liturgy, we need to have at least a priest, a deacon, and one person representing the congregation. So it will be the community, the communal service, the communal work, the work of the people, to be a fellowship together. Through the fellowship comes the knowledge. For example, when a group of youth has fellowship together, they will get to know each other. Without having this fellowship, it will be difficult to know each other.

The Two Aspects of Fellowship

St. John said, "That which we have seen and heard we declare to you, that you also may have fellowship with us; and truly our fellowship is with the Father and with His Son Jesus Christ."[3] The fellowship that St. John speaks about has two important aspects: fellowship with one another and fellowship with the Holy Trinity. Through this fellowship, we will know one another in Christ, and we will also know the Holy Trinity. It is impossible to know the Holy Trinity away from the Liturgy. This is why we, as Orthodox, do not call it Mass, which is a Roman Catholic term coming from a Latin word meaning dismissal; rather, we call it Liturgy, to emphasize the fellowship that is important and foundational in the Liturgy.

St. John said, "If we walk in the light as He is in the light, we have fellowship with one another, and the blood of Jesus Christ His Son cleanses us from all sin."[4] So what is the relationship between fellowship with one another and the blood of Jesus Christ that cleanses us from all sins? Here is the relationship: the blood of Jesus cleanses and purifies us. Then, when we are purified and we are cleansed, we can have fellowship with one another and with the Holy Trinity, in the Holy Trinity. St. Paul said, "And what communion has light with darkness?"[5] That is why St. John said, "If we

---

3   1 John 1:3.
4   1 John 1:7.
5   2 Corinthians 6:14.

walk in the light." If some of us are in darkness because of sin, they cannot have fellowship with people who are righteous and walk in the light. How can this group have fellowship with that group? The blood of Jesus will cleanse them from all sins, from the darkness, and then they walk in the light, and if they walk in the light, they will have fellowship with the light in Jesus Christ. So, in the Liturgy, because all of us are sinners but with the life of repentance and with Communion, the blood of Jesus Christ cleanses us from all sins, and then we will have fellowship with one another, and at the same time we will have fellowship with the Holy Trinity.

Fellowship with Others is Required

Can a person have a fellowship with God (with the Holy Trinity) without having fellowship with one another? Some people say that there is what we call individual piety or individual godliness. They say, "I do not have to come to church. I have a great relationship with God. Why should I come to church? There is no need for me to come to church." When the churches were closed, although we needed to accommodate the situation, many people started to advocate and preach individual piety and individual godliness. "Yes, you can be with God alone. The church is not important. Go into the inner room and you yourself pray to God and then you will have fellowship with God, and that is it."

But I am telling you, as St. John said, that we have fellowship with one another and our fellowship with the Holy Trinity. This is why God said that our fellowship is like the body: think about your body, every organ in your body has a relationship with the brain, with the head, and with every single organ. We call it the nervous system. So each organ in your body, through the nervous system, has a relationship with the brain, but also each organ in your body is connected with the rest of your body. That is why if you have an illness in one organ, the whole body will feel the pain because we are connected. And there is a tissue called the connective tissue. What does the connective tissue mean? It is the tissue that connects all the organs of the body, that is, the fellowship. We are connected to one another, and we are connected to the head. But those who advocate individual piety or individual godliness as though there is a brain that connects to the liver, and that is it; the heart connects to the brain, and that is it; the lungs connect to the brain, and that is it. But the liver and the heart and the lung and the spleen are not connected together. Can this make a human body? Can this make a human being? No, that is why Christ said to us, "I am the head; you are the body."[6]

Therefore, we must have fellowship together, and at the same time also we must have fellowship with the head. And the head is Christ. But Christ is the Son of the Father. You cannot have fellowship with the Son

---

6   See Colossians 1:18, 2:19.

without the Father. In the Son we become children to the Father, and the Son abides in the Father and the Father abides in the Son; and the Father and the Son are one with the Holy Spirit. So through this fellowship, we, as the body of Christ, are not only one with the head, that is, Christ, but also with the Father and with the Holy Spirit.

In the thirteenth chapter of the gospel of St. John, the Lord gave His body and blood to His disciples. This is the Eucharist, the Last Supper, or the Mystical Supper. After this, in the seventeenth chapter, when Jesus was praying to the Father, He said, "I in them."[7] How is He in them? Communion; He just gave them His body and His blood. He said to them, "Take, eat; this is My body.... Drink from it, all of you. For this is My blood."[8] So now He is saying to the Father, "I in them"; they ate My body and drank My blood, so they are one with Me. Then He said, "And You in Me,"[9] eternally the Father and the Son are one. See how beautiful, "I in them, and You in Me." So, what is the conclusion? "That they may be made perfect in one, and that the world may know that You have sent Me, and have loved them as You have loved Me."[10]

Therefore, this oneness with the Holy Trinity cannot be achieved outside the Liturgy, outside Communion, outside the Eucharist. Excommunication

---

7 John 17:23.
8 Matthew 26:26–28.
9 John 17:23.
10 Ibid.

is a term used when the Church prevents somebody from partaking of the Eucharist, from taking Communion. Communication means fellowship, oneness, togetherness, so excommunication indicates that a person does not have fellowship—they are not one with us.

The knowledge of the Holy Trinity can be achieved only through the Liturgy and through the Eucharist. In his epistle to the Philippians, St. Paul says, "That I may know Him and the power of His resurrection, and the fellowship of His sufferings, being conformed to His death."[11] So, how can this be achieved? How can we know Him, not with intellectual knowledge but with experiential knowledge? How can we know the power of His resurrection? How can we know the fellowship of His sufferings? And what did He mean by "being conformed to His death"? How can this be achieved in practical terms? Through Communion, through the Liturgy, because in the Liturgy, I will be one with the Son, so I know Him. Before Communion, I am under sentence of death, but after I take Communion, He says to me, "Whoever eats My flesh and drinks My blood has eternal life, and I will raise him up at the last day."[12] Therefore, I will know the power of resurrection and the fellowship of His sufferings in Communion because I am one with the crucified Christ, so this is the fellowship of His sufferings.

---

11   Philippians 3:10.
12   John 6:54.

"Being conformed to His death" is accomplished in Communion, because in communion I die to the world and live to Christ; "it is no longer I who live, but Christ lives in me."[13] That is why St. Paul said to the Corinthians:

> For I received from the Lord that which I also delivered to you: that the Lord Jesus on the same night in which He was betrayed took bread; and when He had given thanks, He broke it and said, "Take, eat; this is My body which is broken for you; do this in remembrance of Me." In the same manner He also took the cup after supper, saying, "This cup is the new covenant in My blood. This do, as often as you drink it, in remembrance of Me." For as often as you eat this bread and drink this cup, you proclaim the Lord's death till He comes.[14]

The last verse that says, "For as often as you eat this bread and drink this cup, you proclaim the Lord's death till He comes," is a key verse, so when we partake of His body and His blood, we live and have fellowship of the sufferings, the death, and the resurrection of Christ.

In the Divine Liturgy, the priest says, "For every time you eat of this bread and drink of this cup, you

---

13 Galatians 2:20.
14 1 Corinthians 11:23–26.

Two Aspects of the Fellowship in the Divine Liturgy

proclaim My Death, confess My Resurrection, and remember Me till I come."[15] Let me remind you of something very beautiful that goes along with what we are saying. So, can I proclaim His death, confess His resurrection, and remember Him without Communion? Intellectually, yes. Without taking Communion, I can say, "Christ died, He rose from the dead, and I will remember Him till His second coming." But you cannot have this fellowship and this knowledge and this proclamation in an experiential way outside of the Liturgy. That is why he said, "Every time you eat of this bread and drink of this cup, you proclaim My Death," because here you experience and have fellowship with the crucified Christ, with His death, with His resurrection, and you remember Him till He comes. The response to this by the congregation is: "Amen. Amen. Amen. Your Death, O Lord, we proclaim; Your holy Resurrection and Ascension into the heavens, we confess." We do not just proclaim intellectually, but rather through experience; it is a real fellowship.

Also, one of the beautiful fractions is the fraction for the feasts of the Virgin and angels, which starts by saying, "Behold Immanuel our God, the Lamb of God who takes away the sin of the whole world, is with us today on this table." Therefore, the greatest activity that we can do in our lives is the Divine Liturgy. There is no greater activity than the Divine Liturgy, because in the Divine Liturgy we have Immanuel, our God, bodily with us on the Altar—His body and His blood.

---

15   The Divine Liturgy of St. Basil – The Institution Narrative.

There is also a hymn called the Bread of Life, in which we say, "Around You stand the cherubim and seraphim, and they cannot look at You. We behold You upon the Altar." So we have a privilege that even the cherubim and seraphim do not have. Not only can we see Him, but we also partake of Him; we become one with Him. His body will become our body, His blood will become our blood. There is no greater activity than the Divine Liturgy. So the Divine Liturgy is the mystery of the fellowship with the Holy Trinity and with one another.

2

How to Achieve Fellowship in the Divine Liturgy

In this chapter, we will speak about eight practical applications concerning how we participate in and actualize the fellowship in the Divine Liturgy.

1. Sharing and Offering Lead to Fellowship

In the early Church, the following practice was prevalent, and I witnessed it when I was a little child. My family was originally not from Cairo but from a city in Upper Egypt. As a little child, during summer vacation, we used to go to my grandfather's house and stay for a few weeks in Upper Egypt. And every Saturday, I remember very well that there was a person who baked the Corban, the bread for the Church. Here, nowadays, volunteers are doing this, but in Egypt, there was one person dedicated to this service.

So I recall that he used to go to all the houses of the believers on Saturday, and each house would give him some flour. From this flour that he collected from all the houses of the believers, he made the Corban, from which the Lamb was chosen for the Divine Liturgy.

So, as a little child, I did not understand why he was doing this. I know there are many rich families, so one family can give him all the flour that is needed instead of him going from house to house to take a little flour from each. So I asked why he was doing this. Just one family can contribute and give him the flour, and the next week another family. Why should he go from one house to another? He even went to the poor families that gave him a small amount of flour. And it was thus explained to me: This was done to have fellowship, so each one will be represented in this bread that is offered on the Altar. From this flour, the bread is made, so everyone is represented in this Corban that will be the body of Christ.

This was the practice of the early Church, but unfortunately, it has disappeared now. This is what St. Paul said, "The cup of blessing which we bless, is it not the communion (the fellowship) of the blood of Christ? The bread which we break, is it not the communion (the fellowship) of the body of Christ? For we, though many, are one bread and one body; for we all partake of that one bread."[16]

---

[16] 1 Corinthians 10:16–17. The words in parentheses are added for clarity.

That is why we do not offer five loaves of bread or five cups, rather only one bread and one cup. It is the fellowship, the communion. Communion means union together.

Now that I told you that this has disappeared, so what is the replacement for this beautiful tradition, and this is the first point on how to have fellowship—true fellowship. So at least when you come to the Liturgy, come with your offering, regardless how little it is, even if it were two cents; when you come to the liturgy come with your offering to the church, each one and not only the father or the mother, but the father, the mother, and the children; each one should come to church with their offering. Even though you pay your tithes once a month through check or online, every time you come to church, come with your offering.

St. Paul says to the Corinthians, "Now concerning the collection for the saints, as I have given orders to the churches of Galatia, so you must do also: On the first day of the week let each one of you lay something aside, storing up as he may prosper, that there be no collections when I come."[17] The Apostle orders them to collect "on the first day of the week." He did not say "on the first day of the month" or "once a year," rather "on the first day of the week," Sunday, that is, each Sunday when you come to the liturgy. And he says, "let each one of you," and did not say "let each family."

---

17   1 Corinthians 16:1.

Therefore, when we come to church, each one of us should come with their offering, whether the offering is one cent, two cents, one dollar, or five dollars: Whatever you can afford. As the Lord in the Old Testament said, "None shall appear before Me empty,"[18] so when the priest prays the Litany for the Oblations, "Remember, O Lord, those who have brought to You these gifts, those on whose behalf they have been brought, and those by whom they have been brought," you will be in one of these groups. And when I bring my offering and you bring your offering, all our offerings will ascend before God as a sweet-smelling aroma—one offering. It will be one offering before God. This is our fellowship and our communion with one another.

2. The Readings of the Divine Liturgy

There are two purposes for the readings in the Church. Let me ask you a question: Was the fifteenth chapter of St. John after or before the Eucharist? After the Eucharist, because the Eucharist was in the thirteenth chapter of St. John. In the fifteenth chapter, Christ says, "You are already clean because of the word which I have spoken to you."[19] The word of God cleansed them. So one of the purposes of the readings is to cleanse us and purify us before partaking of Communion. That is why attending the readings is very important, not

---

18 Exodus 23:15.
19 John 15:3.

only the gospel but all the readings: the psalm and the Gospel of the Raising of Morning Incense, the Pauline epistle, the Catholic epistle, the Praxis (Acts), the psalm and the Gospel of the Liturgy, because they have a role in our cleansing and our purification.

There is, however, another purpose for the readings. When we listen to the same readings together, all of us will have the same mind, and all of us will be thinking about the same thing. Is this unity? Is this a fellowship? Yes, so listening and paying attention to the readings and to the sermon make us have one mind and be in one accord. Therefore, the second practical point of how to achieve fellowship in the Divine Liturgy is by listening and paying attention to the readings.

3. The Holy Kiss and the Reconciliation.

Why has the Church made the holy kiss an essential element in the Divine Liturgy, and the deacon calling everyone to greet one another with a holy kiss? The holy kiss is not a kiss of passion and lust, as we say in The Divine Liturgy of St. Cyril; neither is it a kiss of betrayal, like Judas'. The holy kiss is rather the kiss of reconciliation, as the Lord said, "If you bring your gift to the altar, and there remember that your brother has something against you, leave your gift there before the altar, and go your way. First be reconciled to your brother, and then come and offer your gift."[20]

---

20 Matthew 5:23–24.

When we are reconciled to one another and have peace with one another, this is fellowship. Without this, we cannot have fellowship. And since Communion—the Eucharist—is fellowship, this is why in every Divine Liturgy, the deacon says, "Greet one another with a holy kiss."

Some people try to outsmart God: If I have a conflict with this person and this person is praying in the church of Archangel Michael, I will pray in the church of St. Mary, but this does not work with God. Or if this person is sitting here, I will sit over there. So when the deacon says greet one another, I am avoiding him. Now, greeting one another means the ability to greet any believer with a heart that has no grudges in it, with sincere and genuine love, and with a spirit of reconciliation. You cannot outsmart God, and without this kiss of peace, there is no fellowship.

4. Perseverance

Can I have fellowship with you while I am skipping some Sundays, and you attend all Sundays? When I skip some Liturgies, but you attend all Liturgies, can we have fellowship with one another in this way? We cannot. When we attend the Liturgy regularly and when we come constantly to church, then our fellowship will be actualized; but if I skip one or two Sundays, or come once a month, our fellowship will never be actualized. So in order to actualize our fellowship with one another, we need to attend regularly and not skip any Sunday.

St. Paul spoke about this in his epistle to the Hebrews, saying, "And let us consider one another in order to stir up love and good works, not forsaking the assembling of ourselves together, as is the manner of some, but exhorting one another, and so much the more as you see the Day approaching."[21] St. Paul found some people skipping certain Sundays and not coming to church every Sunday. Therefore, he said, "No, you cannot do this." It is very important to be regular and consistent in attending the Divine Liturgy every Sunday.

5. Participation

Some people come to church as observers. I am standing, watching. I am watching what the priest is doing and what the deacon is doing; and that is it. And perhaps I am watching and judging. I am observing what is going on. This is not liturgy. Liturgy means all of us participate. This is why the "priest says," the "deacon says," and then the "congregation says." So, your participation as a congregation in the chanting and prayer will make us one, united, in fellowship with one another.

Not only that, every now and then the deacon gives you instruction: "Pray for the peace of the one, holy, catholic, and apostolic orthodox Church of God," "Pray for the salvation of the world," "Pray for these holy precious gifts, our sacrifices, and those who

---

21 Hebrews 10:24–25.

bring them," "Pray for perfect peace," "Pray that God may have mercy and compassion on us," and so on.

So when the deacon says, "Pray," you should pray, lifting your heart to God. Unfortunately, in some churches, when they want to finish the service quickly, the deacon skips these responses. I want, however, to say that the intention is beyond these responses; it is not just to repeat what the priest says. No, the priest says, "Remember, O Lord, the peace of Your one, only, holy, catholic, and apostolic Church," and lest the people be distracted, the deacon instructs the people, saying, "You also should pray with the priest," and so the deacon responds after the priest, saying, "Pray for the peace of the one, holy, catholic, and apostolic orthodox Church of God."

Therefore, all of us are praying. When all of us are praying together the same prayer, that is fellowship. That is oneness in mind and oneness in spirit; however, just to be disconnected and watching, observing what is happening, you are not having fellowship. So, fellowship is actualized through the active participation in prayer and chanting in the Divine Liturgy.

6. Avoiding Individual Piety

Although we have already spoken about this, I will repeat it. The meaning of this is that although every one of us should have a personal relationship with God, the fellowship, nevertheless, cannot be actualized without having fellowship with one another. You cannot have fellowship with God without having fellowship with one another. Therefore, do not separate yourself from the spirit of the one, holy, catholic, apostolic Church; catholic here means universal.

Some people have made up their own spiritual rule or canon, for example: I will come to church in the last thirty minutes; I will attend the Liturgy once every month; I will not fast the Fast of the Apostles; I will not fast on Wednesdays and Fridays. So they have their own agenda, their own rule or canon, away from the spirit of the Church. How can we be united and have fellowship with one another while each one has their own rule or canon, their own way of worship?

There is no fellowship in this individual approach to godliness. We read in the Book of Acts the phrase "all with one accord" repeated several times. All of them together in prayer and fasting—this is fellowship. So avoid the individual piety or the individual godliness; you are not individual anymore, but are a member in the body of Christ.

Before Baptism, you were an individual. Individual means indivisible and cannot connect with others, cannot unite with others, cannot have communion with others, cannot have fellowship with others. This is what individual linguistically means. But in Baptism, you are not an individual; you have become a part, an organ, a member in one body, the body of Christ. Can you imagine if an organ is not in harmony, not synchronized with the rest of your body? Can you imagine if your right eye is not synchronized with your left eye? You will see double vision. So you cannot be not synchronized with the body of Christ and say you are a member in the body of Christ. Therefore, avoid individual piety or individual godliness.

7. The Same Sound Dogma, Theology, and Fellowship

There is a Coptic word of Greek origin, *metevsebis* [ⲙⲉⲧⲉⲩⲥⲉⲃⲏⲥ]. The Greek word can be translated into either religion, dogma, doctrine, or godliness. In his epistle to Timothy, St. Paul says, "And without controversy great if the mystery of godliness: God was manifested in the flesh."[22] So what is the link here? What is the mystery of godliness? He is speaking about doctrine here: "God was manifested in the flesh," that is the doctrine of the incarnation of the Son of God. I can read the verse as follows: "Without controversy, great is the mystery of this doctrine: the doctrine of incarnation." Why is this doctrine great? Why did God become man and take flesh—"was incarnate and became man"? Because we failed; all humanity failed to fulfill the righteousness, the righteous requirement of God. So God became man to fulfill all righteousness, the righteous requirement of God, and then the Holy Spirit took from what is His and gave to us.

---

22   1 Timothy 3:16.

So, we receive the righteousness of Christ freely in Baptism and Chrismation. So, His righteousness becomes my righteousness; then I will be godly, because I received the righteousness of Christ. Great is this doctrine of the incarnation of the Son of God because only through this doctrine, I will be godly, be righteous. Without the incarnation of the Son of God, it is impossible for anyone to be righteous—to be godly. That is why the same word can be translated as godliness or religion (doctrine).

Where do we say the same phrase, "the mystery of godliness," in the Divine Liturgy? The Institution Narrative. In the Institution Narrative of The Divine Liturgy of St. Basil, the priest says, "He instituted for us this great mystery of godliness." So this mystery of the incarnation we can now see in the Divine Liturgy, because in the Divine Liturgy "Immanuel our God … is with us today on this table,"[23] bodily by His body and blood. That is why we call the Liturgy, the mystery of incarnation or the mystery of godliness.

Can we partake of His body and His blood if the Son of God did not become incarnate? No. So His incarnation, this doctrine, made it possible that we partake of His body and His blood, and when we partake of His body and blood, the priest at the end of the Liturgy says, "Given for us for salvation, remission of sins, and eternal life to those who partake of Him," that is godliness, remission of sins, salvation, eternal

---

23 Fraction to the Father for the Feasts of the Virgin and Angels.

life. So, how do we have fellowship? When we have the same doctrine, the same theology, one faith, one body, but if we do not have the same faith, it is not impossible to have unity.

Some people say, "No, doctrine splits us into different denominations; just put the doctrines aside and let us be one." You cannot. The doctrine will make us godly, and through this godliness, you can be one. So if we do not have the same doctrine, then we cannot be godly, and if we are not godly, we cannot be one. That is why it is very important to have the same doctrine—the same faith. There is no unity without the same faith: one faith, one body; one faith, true fellowship.

8. Partaking of the Same Body and Blood

And the last point, which is most obvious, but I kept it to the end, is Communion. You cannot have fellowship without taking Communion. When we take Communion from the same Body and drink the same Blood, so His Body is in me and each one of you, then all of us will be one whether the person is in Arizona, in Texas, in Florida; in America, in Egypt, in Australia, in Canada; in Africa or in Asia. We are partaking of the same Body, drinking from the same cup, so we become one.

Concluding Remarks on Fellowship

Therefore, to actualize this fellowship, this oneness, in the Divine Liturgy, we need to participate and become one through offering; listening to the Church readings; the holy kiss and the reconciliation; the regular attendance every week to the Divine Liturgy; the actual participation in the Divine Liturgy, in praising and in praying; avoidance of individual piety or individual godliness; having the same faith, sound doctrine, and sound teaching because that is the mystery of godliness or the mystery of religion; and finally partaking of the same body and blood.

God gave us His body and His blood to be one with one another and one with the Holy Trinity. This oneness cannot be actualized without the Divine Liturgy, so let me conclude this chapter with what the priest prays in the introduction for the Litany of Peace, which he prays after the descent of the Holy Spirit. The priest prays, saying, "Make us all worthy, O our Master, to partake of your Holies, unto the purification of our souls, bodies, and spirits," but is this purification the ultimate goal? No, Communion leads to godliness and purification, but this is not the ultimate goal. What is the ultimate goal? The priest continues, saying, "That we may become one body and one spirit, and may have a share and inheritance with all the saints who have pleased You since the beginning"—that is, fellowship with one another, fellowship with the saints, and fellowship with God because we are partaking of His body and His blood, and He is one with the Father and the Holy Spirit.

Again, if you come to the Liturgy with the intention of just taking Communion for your purification and salvation, you are short-sighted; that is not the ultimate goal. The ultimate goal is fellowship, which is why we call it communion. The purification is just a transition, so we partake of His body and His blood to be purified that we may become one body and one spirit, and we have a share and inheritance with all the saints who have pleased God since the beginning. Therefore, the ultimate goal is fellowship with the Holy Trinity, fellowship with one another, and fellowship with the saints who departed and pleased God since the beginning.

3

A Brief Explanation of the Structure of the Liturgy

You know that when the Lord appeared to the two disciples of Emmaus, He explained to them, as we read in the gospel of St. Luke, from Moses and all the Books what pertains to Him. Then they went to the house, and He broke the bread, and their eyes were opened to recognize Him after He broke the bread. Therefore, before breaking the bread and their eyes being opened, the Lord explained to them from all the Books what pertained to Him. That is why the Church incorporated a message about the Lord Jesus Christ in the readings, which are between the Thanksgiving Prayer and the Institution Narrative.

The Divine Liturgy follows the exact steps that the Lord did on Thursday. Let us review the steps: He took bread, He gave thanks, He blessed it, He sanctified it,

He broke it, He gave it, then they praised God and left for the Mount of Olives. These are the seven steps. This is the structure of the Divine Liturgy. He took bread, that is, the offering of the Lamb. Then He gave thanks, that is, the Thanksgiving Prayer. He blessed it, that is, the Institution Narrative. He sanctified, that is, the calling of the Holy Spirit to descend upon the elements. He broke it, that is, the Fraction. He gave it, that is, Communion. They praised God, which is why we chant Psalm 150 at the end. So, these are the seven stages of the Divine Liturgy, following exactly the steps that the Lord Jesus Christ instituted on Covenant Thursday.

The Divine Liturgy: A Journey from the Old Testament to the New Testament

The Divine Liturgy takes us on a journey from the Old Testament to the New Testament. We can say that there are four stages in the manifestation of the Son of God, our Lord Jesus Christ, to us.

The First Stage: The Hidden Messiah

The first stage, the hidden Messiah, is in the Offering of the Morning and Evening Incense. We notice that the priest is standing outside the altar, and when he enters inside the altar, he usually enters with incense, in a cloud of incense, in order to symbolize that Jesus is hidden—the Messiah is hidden. Besides this cloud, He is not revealed yet, and that is why in the Old Testament, the altar of incense was outside the Holy of Holies. So the Offering of the Morning and Evening Incense were outside the Holy of Holies, outside the altar.

One of the common mistakes is that the priest would be standing outside, but the deacon stands inside. If the priest is standing outside, then the deacon should also be standing outside, holding a cross and standing behind the priest. That is where the deacon should stand in the Offering of the Morning and Evening Incense. And when the priest enters into the altar, the deacon should enter with him, to do the procession around the altar; and this is with a cloud of incense.

The Second Stage: Baby Jesus

In the second stage, Jesus is born. This is in the Offering of the Lamb when the priest chooses the lamb and then he wraps it as St. Mary wrapped Baby Jesus in swaddling cloths. In the Offering of the Lamb, we demonstrate that Jesus was born in the fullness of time from St. Mary. And then we end this when the priest prays the absolution of the servants and covers the altar.

The Third Stage: Jesus the Teacher

In this stage, because the lamb is covered, we must have the gospel, because it symbolizes Jesus the Teacher. So the gospel should be clear during the reading of the Pauline epistle, the Catholic epistle, and during all the readings. And this is the Liturgy of the Catechumens: teaching and preaching.

The Fourth Stage: Jesus the Sacrifice

Then the fourth stage is at the beginning of the Liturgy of the Faithful when the priest lifts the prospheron[24]. This is when the deacon takes the gospel and puts it behind the throne and the chalice, because now Jesus ended His teaching, as we read about on Holy Tuesday in Passion Week. He left the temple and did not teach anymore; that was on Tuesday. He rested on Great Wednesday. Then on Covenant Thursday, He established the Eucharist and was crucified on Great Friday. That is why we take the gospel and put it behind the chalice—behind, because we have now lifted the prospheron and have Jesus the Sacrifice.

---

24 Prospheron is the large white cloth that covers the entire Altar after the Thanksgiving Prayer to the start of the Anaphora.

4

How to Prepare Myself for the Divine Liturgy

Before the Divine Liturgy

At Home

It starts from the night before the Divine Liturgy. That is why we start with the Offering of Evening Incense on Saturday for Sunday's Divine Liturgy. If you can attend the Offering of Evening Incense and Midnight Praises, that would be wonderful, but if your circumstances do not allow, at least this night, you need to pray before going to sleep. Every night you should surely pray, but this night in particular, do not skip prayer for any reason. Ask God to prepare you for the Divine Liturgy, which you will attend.

You need to sleep early so that you can wake up early and come early to church. The Offering of

Morning Incense is not for the priest only; it is for all of us. Therefore, from the time the priest starts praying, all of us should be there. But if you stayed up late the night before, the next day you will be tired, and you will get up late, and you will not have time even to pray before you come to church. If you sleep early, however, on that night, then on the day of the Liturgy, you will wake up early and will also have time to pray before you leave and come to church. Do not say, "I am going to pray in church, and it is enough."

In the Book of Psalms, there are psalms called Psalms of Ascents. "Ascent" comes from the word "ascending." Because the temple was on a mountain, people would ascend the mountain, so before going to the top of the mountain, to the temple to pray, while they were ascending the mountain, they were praying. That is why the Church teaches us to pray before we come to church.

And we need to ask God to teach us how to pray and how to stand before Him to offer Him the appropriate doxology. It is also good to open the Scripture and read the readings of the day before you come to church. This will prepare you for the theme, and if you can find out the theme that connects all these readings, then this will help you enjoy the readings.

On the Way

And on your way to church, you need to keep your mind holy and godly. You may pray some psalms like, "I was glad for those who said to me, 'We will go into the house of the Lord,'"[25] and, "One thing I have asked of the Lord, this also I will seek, that I should dwell in the house of the Lord all the days of my life."[26] And yet another psalm says, "Blessed is the man You choose, and cause to approach You, that he may dwell in Your courts. We shall be satisfied with the goodness of Your house."[27]

Keep your mind in a state of prayer. Then, when you arrive at church, say, "How beloved are Your dwellings, O Lord, God of hosts!"[28] And you can come and bow down, kneeling in front of the altar; or if you cannot do this, you can take your seat, make the sign of the cross, and say, "I worship You, O Christ, with Your good Father and the Holy Spirit, for You have come and saved us." Then you can pray the psalm from the Eleventh Hour, "Unto You I have lifted up my eyes, O You who dwell in heaven."[29] All these prayers will put you in the mood for prayer. And you should come to church without eating or drinking, even if you are not going to take Communion, to be fasting and praying.

---

25 Psalm 121 (The Eleventh Hour of the Agpeya).

26 Psalm 26 (The First Hour of the Agpeya).

27 Psalms 65:4.

28 Psalm 83 (The Sixth Hour of the Agpeya).

29 Psalm 122 (The Eleventh Hour of the Agpeya).

Bring an offering

St. Paul tells us in his first epistle to the Corinthians that we need to come with our offering. As the Lord also said, "None shall appear before Me empty,"[30] Even though you pay your tithe by sending a check every month or however you do so, it is also good to offer something, even if it is just 50 cents or one dollar.

St. Paul said, "Now concerning the collection for the saints, as I have given orders to the churches of Galatia, so you must do also: On the first day of the week let each one of you lay something aside, storing up as he may prosper, that there be no collections when I come."[31] By "the first day of the week," he means Sunday, that is, on Sunday because it is the day of worship. By "let each one of you," he means adults and children, both male and female; everybody should "lay something aside, storing up, as he may prosper." So here St. Paul is teaching us that on every Sunday when we worship, each one should put something aside, even if you usually pay your tithes electronically or by mailing a check. You need to come with your offering to church, with whatever you can afford.

---

30 Exodus 23:15.
31 1 Corinthians 16:1.

During the Divine Liturgy

Following the Instructions of the Liturgy

Many times, the deacon says, "Let us attend." This means pay attention. So the deacon is instructing us several times to pay attention during the prayer, because we are tempted to get distracted. The deacon also gives us many instructions. For example, when he says, "Pray for the peace of the one, holy, catholic, and apostolic orthodox Church of God," are you praying for the peace of the Church? This is an instruction for you. When the deacon says, "Pray for our archpriest, Pope Abba Tawadros II … and for our orthodox bishops," are you praying? When he says, "Pray for the salvation of the world and this city of ours," are you praying? So all these are instructions, which you need to respond to, and to interact with, and to pray, lifting your heart in prayer. "Pray for prefect peace, love, and the holy apostolic greetings." You need to lift your heart and pray when the deacon gives you instructions to pray.

Appropriate Conduct Before God

We say in the Divine Liturgy, "Before whom stand the angels, the archangels, the principalities, the authorities, the thrones, the dominions, and the powers,"[32] and, "The cherubim and the seraphim… with two they cover their faces and with two they cover their feet."[33]

---

32 The Divine Liturgy of St. Basil – Anaphora.
33 The Divine Liturgy of St. Gregory – Anaphora.

Unfortunately, many people just walk in and out during the Divine Liturgy for no reason. A deacon, for example, gets bored, so he decides to go out and walk, to leave the church, to take a break, and then come back. Is it appropriate? Of course, it is inappropriate. Some girls find themselves bored, so they leave, go and talk together, and then come back.

When we were young, deacons in middle school and high school, I remember our priest told us that even if there is a fire in the church, we should not move to put it out. To that extent, they taught us to be serious, how to stand in church during the Divine Liturgy, with that reverence that befits God.

Walking back and forth for no reason, however, is unacceptable. Some people are now texting and checking their phones several times for no reason, when we need to eliminate distractions. It is perhaps better to turn your phone completely off, or if you are following the prayers on your phone, put it on Airplane Mode, so you do not get distracted when you are praying in church.

Participation is Key

Another thing is that you need not be an observer but a participant. Some people come to the Liturgy just to watch what is happening, but people should rather be participants. All of us know how to say, "Amen. Amen. Amen," "Through the intercession," and "The cherubim." Why do you only leave the deacons to chant? Why are you not participating? It is written "the congregation says." So you need to participate. I remember back in our churches in Egypt when we chanted "Amen. Amen. Amen," or "The cherubim," or "Through the intercession," everybody used to participate, and you would feel the church shaking from the power of prayer.

Here, however, you find a few people chanting, and the rest are watching. When you participate, you will not feel bored, but you will feel bored if you come with the wrong mindset: "I need to take Communion. Why is the priest saying this? Why is it taking too long?" That will make you feel more bored and distracted, but if you come with the right mindset, to enjoy every part of the Liturgy and to pray, you will never get bored.

Let me share with you something funny about me. When I was little, at the end of the Liturgy, when the deacons say, "Amen. Alleluia. Doxa Patri,"[34] I thought that the deacons were upset because the priest ended the Liturgy, so they wanted him to prolong it more. For a very long time, when I was little, I thought that the deacons were not saying, "Amen. Alleluia. Doxa Patri," but rather they were saying, "Amen. Alleluia. Lissa Badri."[35] It is still early; why are you finishing the Liturgy now? We want to stay more. So when you

---

34 "Amen. Alleluia. Glory to the Father…"
35 The phrase "Glory to the Father" in Coptic sounds similar to the Arabic "It is still early."

come and participate, you will find it still early. You would want to stay longer in church. When you sit with somebody very close to you and you love them, you do not want to leave; you feel that time is flying.

During Communion

Reverence during Communion is another point to consider. The time of Communion and distribution in many churches is the time of chaos in the church. People are walking in every direction; people are greeting one another; people are checking text messages and emails, as if the Liturgy is over. Although the time of distribution is the holiest time in the Divine Liturgy. Here, our sacrificial Lamb is giving us His body and His blood for the forgiveness of our sins and eternal life. In what mindset and in what condition should we receive His body and His blood? Can you imagine: He broke His body to give us life? Therefore, this is a time of reverence and prayer and joy and praise: "Praise God in all His saints," not talk with one another, and greet one another. This is not a time for greeting and talking; it is a time for praising God.

After the Divine Liturgy

And after the Liturgy, I know now we have the Agape [gathering], but in the Paradise of Holy Fathers, there is the following story:

> Abba Macarius the Great used to say to the brothers at Scete when he was dismissing the congregation: "Flee, brothers!" One of the elders said to him: "Where can we flee to that is more remote than this desert?" and he placed his finger on his mouth, saying: "Flee from this," and he went into his own cell, shut the door, and stayed there.[36]

After Liturgy, it is not time to gossip, to judge, to speak negatively about one another. As Christians, we should not do that at any time, but unfortunately, frequently, when you go to the Agape Hall, it becomes for some a time to discuss church politics, to gossip about one another, to criticize the negatives, and to badmouth. Is this Agape? Agape means love. So we need to say something edifying. Maybe we can read, talk about the readings of today, what revelation or manifestation we learned today in the Liturgy, and how God manifested Himself to me? Talk about something edifying.

---

36 *Give Me a Word: The Alphabetical Sayings of the Desert Fathers*, Wortley J., trans. (Yonkers, NY: SVS Press, 2014), Macarius the Egyptian 16.

5

In the Divine Liturgy, I Understand...

The following reflections perhaps revolved in the mind and heart of the saint Pope Kyrillos VI, making him ardently love the Divine Liturgy.

A Sacrifice of Love

In the Divine Liturgy, we find ourselves standing before a sacrifice of love. "Greater love has no one than this, than to lay down one's life for his friends."[37] The love of God was made manifest in the breaking of His body for our sakes. When we stand in the Divine Liturgy and see His blood that is shed and His body that is broken, we discover the mystery of love in the sacrifice of the cross. The sacrifice of the cross is an embodiment of the divine love, which we clearly see in the Divine Liturgy.

---

37 John 15:13.

In the Divine Liturgy, I Understand...

St. John says, "Now before the Feast of the Passover, when Jesus knew that His hour had come that He should depart from this world to the Father, having loved His own who were in the world, He loved them to the end."[38] This love, which is to the end, we see in the sacrifice of the Divine Liturgy. This love turned into a desire in the heart of our Lord, that He break His body. Thus He—glory be to Him—said, "With fervent desire I have desired to eat this Passover with you before I suffer."[39] Love for us turned in the heart of our Lord into a desire that He offer Himself as a sacrifice and break His body for the sake of our salvation.

For this reason, we meet this desire of love with a desire to partake of the body of the Lord and His blood. We see that He desired to offer Himself a sacrifice for our sakes, so we come that we may unite with this Body that is broken and this Blood that is shed. Therefore, the worship in the Divine Liturgy is a desire of love.

For this reason, the martyrs participated in the sacrifice of the Divine Liturgy, so that they offered themselves a sacrifice of love upon the altar of love for the sake of the One who offered His life a sacrifice of love for our sakes. In the past, it was necessary that part of the relics or bones of the martyrs be placed under the altar. The foundation of the altar is the remains of the martyrs. This is taken from the Book

---

38 John 13:1.
39 Luke 22:15.

of Revelation: "I saw under the altar the souls of those who had been slain for the word of God and for the testimony which they held."[40]

When we see the love of our Lord and that He desires to be sacrificed for our sakes, which we see and live in the Divine Liturgy, this makes us also ready to give ourselves for the sake of God—to give ourselves to the point of death and martyrdom. St. Ignatius of Antioch, who was the Bishop of Antioch and a disciple of St. John the Beloved, said the following when the people wanted to prevent him from being martyred. He answered them in a beautiful epistle, saying, "Suffer me to become food for the wild beasts, through whose instrumentality it will be granted me to attain to God. I am the wheat of God, and let me be ground by the teeth of the wild beasts, that I may be found the pure bread of Christ."[41] Therefore, man, who offers himself a sacrifice of love to God, becomes himself the altar.

St. Paul confirms this meaning of worship [or service to God], saying, "I beseech you therefore, brethren, by the mercies of God, that you present your bodies a living sacrifice, holy, acceptable to God, which is your reasonable service."[42] When I come to worship our Lord in the Divine Liturgy, I offer myself a sacrifice. For this reason, I come to Liturgy fasting, and remain standing in fear and trembling, and come with reverence. I offer myself a sacrifice to God,

---

40   Revelation 6:9.
41   St. Ignatius of Antioch, *Epistle to the Romans* 4. (ANF[1]).
42   Romans 12:1.

because I see that the sacrifice of love is made manifest in the Body and Blood which are on the Altar. And from here, I offer myself "a living sacrifice, holy, acceptable to God, which is your reasonable service."

The Manifestation of the Mystical Body of the Lord

What does the manifestation of the mystical body of the Lord mean? It means that we meet the Body on the paten and the Blood in the chalice, and after we receive Communion, the body of the Lord disappears completely from atop the Altar. Nothing at all remains on the paten, not even a pearl,[43] nor in the chalice. So, where is the body of our Lord? We become the invisible body of the Lord through Communion, because we partake of the body of the Lord and His blood. The body of the Lord completely disappears from atop the Altar, so that He may live in our lives, so we become His mystical body.

We eat the body of the Lord that is broken—"Take, eat; this is My body which is broken for you"[44]— because we live bearing the cross. As we eat the Body that is sacrificed for the sake of the world and drink the Blood that is shed for the sake of the life of the world, in this way, each one of us bears their cross. We eat the Body that is broken because we bear the cross,

---

43 Pearl means any part of the body of the Lord, no matter how small.

44 1 Corinthians 11:24.

and we drink the precious Blood so that "the blood of Jesus Christ His Son cleanses us from all sin."[45] As St. Paul explained, saying, "That He might present her [i.e. the church] to Himself a glorious church, not having spot or wrinkle or any such thing, but that she should be holy and without blemish."[46]

If I understood that in the Divine Liturgy I participate of the sacrifice of the cross, I would understand why our Lord said to us, "For as often as you eat this bread and drink this cup, you proclaim the Lord's death till He comes."[47] We also say in the Divine Liturgy, "For every time you eat of this bread and drink of this cup, you proclaim My Death, confess My Resurrection, and remember Me till I come."[48] Why do we proclaim the death of the Lord? Because I participate in bearing the cross. We also confess His resurrection, so I have become a member in the body of Christ that suffered, the body of Christ that is broken.

What is the suffering of the mystical body of Christ? It is the suffering of Its members, that is, ours, because we are the members of the body of Christ, wrestling with the world against sin, wrestling unto bloodshed against sin.[49] These are the sufferings of the martyrs and confessors at the hand of the persecutors of the Church; the sufferings of those who fight in the

---

45 1 John 1:7.
46 Ephesians 5:27.
47 1 Corinthians 11:26.
48 The Divine Liturgy of St. Basil – the Institution Narrative.
49 See Hebrews 12:4.

spiritual warfare against the demons and the spiritual powers of evil in the heavens; the sufferings of the spiritually sick members, from whose sicknesses tumors arise that incline to the world. So the mystical body of Christ, which is the Church, and its head is Christ, carries these sufferings, sins, and evils. For this reason, as the priest chooses the lamb, he says, "We ask You, O Lamb of God, who carries the sin of the world."

If we understood that in the Liturgy and by Communion I share with the suffering body of Christ, then my running away from carrying the cross would be my separation from the crucified, suffering body of Christ. If I run away from humiliation and hardship, then I am separated from the body of Christ. This made Abba Paul the first hermit say, "He who runs away from hardship runs away from God." For the cross is our life, and he who separates from the cross separates from the sacrificed body of Christ. This made St. Paul the Apostle say, "I bear in my body the marks of the Lord Jesus."[50] And these marks are nothing but suffering. "If anyone desires to come after Me, let him deny himself, and take up his cross, and follow Me."[51] In the Divine Liturgy, we see His body that is broken, and the priest, during the Fraction, breaks this body, and we see His blood that is shed, and so I know that I am a member in the suffering body of Christ.

---

50 Galatians 6:17.
51 Matthew 16:24.

The Life of Humility

In the Divine Liturgy, I also understand the meaning of the life of humility. In the Liturgy, I am not an individual nor a being, but rather I am a mere member in the body of Christ: Christ is the head of the Church, and we are all members in the body of Christ. If I can still sense my ego, my dignity, and my independent entity, then it means that I have been separated from the body of Christ, because egotism and pride are a withered branch that has become isolated from the head. As our Lord said, "I am the vine, you are the branches.... If anyone does not abide in Me, he is cast out as a branch and is withered."[52] If I can still sense my ego, then I have become a branch separated from the vine that dries up, withers, and dies. As for humility, it is a branch that abides in the body of Christ.

For this reason, in Communion, I live the self-sacrifice, because I completely vanish; I am a mere member in the body of Christ. Sometimes in Communion, we receive a very small pearl, so I am like this small pearl. My life, however, is that I be in the body of Christ. In Communion, I completely vanish, so I live in Christ who is the head; I live as a mere member united with the rest of the members. Therefore, after Communion, I can say, "It is no longer I who live, but Christ lives in me."[53] In Communion, I learn humility and understand what humility is.

---

52   John 15:5–6.
53   Galatians 2:20.

Intercession

In the Divine Liturgy, the meaning of intercession is made clear. The people who do not understand the concept of intercession do not understand the Divine Liturgy. All of us are members in the body of Christ, not only those who are on earth, but even those who have departed. The Virgin St. Mary, the martyrs, the saints, and all of us who are still on the earth are members in the one body. If one of the members suffers, the whole body suffers; if one member is honored, all the members rejoice. When we celebrate the feast of a saint, like St. John the Baptist and Pope Kyrillos VI, all the people are joyful, chanting hymns of praise. This is because we are members in the same body; we are all in one loaf of bread that is the body of Christ.

Therefore, the member who abides in the body of the Lord understands the meaning of intercession. He prays for the sake of the rest of the members and seeks their prayers, whether these members are in heaven or on earth. For this reason, we pray for the sake of the saints: We pray for St. Mary, St. John the Baptist, St. Stephen, and Pope Kyrillos VI. We say in the Divine Liturgy, "Graciously accord, O Lord, to remember all the saints who have pleased You since the beginning.... Most of all, the pure, full-of-glory, ever-virgin, holy Theotokos, Saint Mary." We pray for them, and they, in turn, pray for us. We pray for them in the Commemoration of the Saints in the Divine Liturgy, and we seek their prayers in the Commemoration of the Saints in

Midnight Praises, in the Hymn of the Intercessions, in the Verses of Cymbals, and in the Doxologies. So there is a reciprocal prayer, but where does this reciprocal prayer come from? Because we understand that all of us are members in one body, whether those who have departed or those who are still on earth. Therefore, we should not find it strange and say, "Why is there a need for something called intercession?" We are all members; if a member suffers, the rest suffer, and if a member is honored, the rest rejoice with them.

Love for Sinners

In the Divine Liturgy, I also learn what it means to love sinners and to endure the weaknesses of sinners. If there are members in the body that are sick, suffering from the sicknesses of sin, the whole body suffers, and even the head suffers, that is, Christ. Who of us, nevertheless, when his physical body is suffering, hates it? We strive to treat it. Likewise, when there are members that are suffering and are sick with the sickness of sin, I ought to love them, knowing that I too am a sinner like them, and ought to endure them and strive for the sake of their comfort and their healing from all the sicknesses of sin. This leads to the peace and joy of the whole body, and joy in heaven, and all the more the joy of God in one sinner returning. How do we understand this from the Divine Liturgy? I see myself that I am a mere small pearl in the body of Christ, a member in the body of Christ.

In the Divine Liturgy, I Understand...

Salt and Light

In the Divine Liturgy, I understand the meaning of the Lord Christ's saying to me, "You are the salt of the earth.... You are the light of the world."[54] In the Divine Liturgy, when I abide in the Lord, who is the light of the world, the Divine light explodes in my life and the lives of the rest of the members, and so we too become the light of the world. Our Lord said, "I am the light of the world,"[55] and, "You are the light of the world."[56] It is impossible for this to be fulfilled without uniting with each other in the body of Christ in the Liturgy. Not only did He say, "You are the light of the world," He also said, "The righteous will shine forth as the sun in the kingdom of their Father."[57]

The Communion of the Holy Spirit

In the Divine Liturgy, I experience the communion of the Holy Spirit. The priest says, "The love of God the Father, the grace of the only begotten Son ... and the communion and gift of the Holy Spirit." Why does he say, "the communion of the Holy Spirit"? Because the Holy Spirit is the One who gives me the body of Christ in Communion; the Holy Spirit is the One who descends upon the bread and wine, and upon us, in the Divine Liturgy, and gives us the body of Christ.

---

54 Matthew 5:13–14.
55 John 8:12.
56 Matthew 5:14.
57 Matthew 13:43.

So I abide in Christ, and what does this mean, abiding in Christ? Christ is the Son, so I become a son of God the Father. This sonship is actualized in the Divine Liturgy through partaking of the body of the Lord and His blood.

The Lord said about the Holy Spirit, "He will take of what is Mine and declare it to you."[58] When I unite with Christ in Communion, in the Divine Liturgy, the Holy Spirit takes of what is Christ's and gives it to me; that is, He gives me the power of the resurrection of Christ, the purity of Christ, the meekness of Christ, the love of Christ for sinners, the endurance of Christ for evildoers, prayer for the sake of others as Christ prayed for the sake of others, death to the world as Christ died, the refusal to accept glory from men, as Christ declared, saying, "I do not receive honor from men."[59] In the Friday Theotokia, we say, "He took what is ours, and gave us what is His." He took our sins and bore them in His body, and He gave us His holiness and righteousness, and in this way, we bear the fruit of the Spirit in our lives, because I became a branch abiding in the vine. "Abide in Me, and I in you. As the branch cannot bear fruit of itself, unless it abides in the vine, neither can you, unless you abide in Me."[60] And the One who makes me abide in Christ is the Holy Spirit in the Mystery of Communion.

---

58 John 16:14.
59 John 5:41.
60 John 15:4.

In the Divine Liturgy, I Understand…

Obtaining the Power to Die to Sin

In the Divine Liturgy, I obtain the power of death—death, however, to sin and to the world. This is because in the Divine Liturgy I unite with the sacrificed body of Christ, and when I unite with the sacrificed body of Christ, I receive the mystery of the power of death. Therefore, I die to my ego, to pride, to the love of praise, to judging others, to the lack of love, to the lusts of the flesh, to the love of the world. "For every time you eat of this bread and drink of this cup, you proclaim My Death."[61] Why am I proclaiming the death of Christ? Because I have experienced this power of death in my life.

This death is different from restraint and deprivation. For when I die to the lusts of the flesh, I am not in a struggle with the lusts of the flesh, trying to restrain them, feeling deprived. This mystery of the power of death is a divine power. As for restraint and deprivation, this is an inner struggle. In the Divine Liturgy, I sacrifice my will and sacrifice my ego, as the Lord Christ said in Gethsemane, "Not My will, but Yours, be done."[62] The slaughter of the will is accomplished in the Divine Liturgy. For this reason, there are two very beautiful passages—if we understand them—in The Divine Liturgy of St. Gregory. The first passage says, "You have come to the

---

61 The Divine Liturgy of St. Basil – the Institution Narrative.
62 Luke 22:42.

slaughter as a sheep, even to the Cross."[63] He looks to Christ who came to the slaughter, "led as a lamb to the slaughter";[64] "not My will, but Yours, be done."[65] In the passage after this, seeing the sacrificed Christ, and I am uniting with the sacrificed Christ, the priest says, "I offer You, O my Master, the symbols of my freedom."[66] I say to Him, "Lord, I will be part of You; therefore, I offer You, O my Master, the symbols of my freedom." What does this mean? It means that I have no freedom, no will, no opinion. I offer all my will to You: This is the slaughter of the self.

As I saw Christ coming to the slaughter as a sheep, so do I also, by uniting with Christ, offer to Him myself a sacrifice: "I offer You, O my Master, the symbols of my freedom." Therefore, I no longer have my own will. For this reason, the statement after this says, "I write my works according to Your sayings."[67] I no longer have a will, for I will perform Your commandments. I will have perfect obedience to the commandment of the Gospel. Therefore, in the Divine Liturgy, I obtain this power of death to the will, to the love of the world, to sin. Slaughtering the old man, so "it is no longer I who live, but Christ lives in me."[68]

---

63 The Divine Liturgy of St. Gregory – Holy.
64 Isaiah 53:7.
65 Luke 22:42.
66 The Divine Liturgy of St. Gregory – The Institution Narrative.
67 Ibid.
68 Galatians 2:20.

In the Divine Liturgy, I Understand…

Heaven Opening onto the Earth

In the Divine Liturgy, heaven opens onto the earth. Heaven and earth became one, as we say in the hymn "Let us Praise" which is sung during the Fast of the Apostles: "He made the two into one, that is the heaven and the earth." In the sacrifice of the Divine Liturgy, we look onto heaven, and heaven looks onto us. Therefore, in the Divine Liturgy, we live outside the boundaries of place and time, welded to eternity. For this reason, the priest says, "This is the life-giving Flesh that Your only begotten Son, our Lord, God, and Savior Jesus Christ, took from our Lady, the Lady of us all, the holy Theotokos, Saint Mary."[69] It is this He who "confessed the good confession before Pontius Pilate."[70] How? Because I am no longer under time in the Divine Liturgy; these are moments from eternity. And for this reason, I can unite with Christ who was crucified in time, 2000 years ago, and within the boundaries of place. For in the United States, people pray; in Australia, people pray; in Egypt, in Africa, in Europe, people pray. It is the same Sacrifice. The Divine Liturgy takes me out of the boundaries of time and place and unites me to heaven in eternity.

In the litanies of the Third Hour in the Agpeya, it says, "Whenever we stand in Your holy sanctuary, we are considered standing in heaven." When man was expelled from the Garden of Eden, God found man

---

69 The Divine Liturgy of St. Basil – The Confession.
70 Ibid.

on the earth longing for heaven; therefore, our Lord gave us His body and blood on earth, so that we may live through Them as though we were in heaven. He gave us the Divine Liturgy, so that in it we may go out of the boundaries of the earth, and time and place, as though we were in heaven.

In the Divine Liturgy, the Holy Trinity is present. Our Lord is present, of course, in every place and every time, but this is a special presence. For the Church says, "Immanuel our God is now in our midst, with the glory of His Father and the Holy Spirit."[71] And of course, when the Holy Trinity is present, the angels and saints are with Him. Therefore, when we are lazy during the prayer of the Divine Liturgy, we deprive ourselves and the church from honoring and glorifying the Holy Trinity; we deprive the angels from the joy of being present with us; we deprive ourselves, the sinners, from receiving mercy in the Divine Liturgy; we deprive the believers from the divine help; we deprive the departed from our prayers for their sake to complete their repose.

During the Divine Liturgy, the angels and saints are in attendance around the Altar. In the "Great Greet One Another," the deacon says, "O clergy and all the people, with prayer and thanksgiving, with dignity and silence, raise your eyes toward the East: To see the Altar, and the Body and Blood of Immanuel our God placed upon it. The angels and archangels are standing, the seraphim with six wings and the cherubim full of eyes

---

71   The Conclusion of the Adam Theotokia.

are covering their faces because of the splendor of His great glory, which is invisible and ineffable." When I hear these words, that the angels are standing, "with two [wings] they cover their faces and with two they cover their feet,"[72] the reverential presence of the angels before the throne of God instills reverence and the fear of God in our hearts as we attend the Divine Liturgy. For this reason, the deacon cries out and says, "Worship God in fear and trembling."[73]

In the Divine Liturgy, because the angels are present, a very beautiful exchange takes place. We sing with the angels: "Let us praise with the angels, saying, 'Glory to God in the highest, peace on earth, and good will toward men.' We praise You, we bless You, we serve You,"[74] and we say, "The cherubim worship You, and the seraphim glorify You, proclaiming and saying, Holy, holy, holy, Lord of hosts, heaven and earth are full of Your holy glory."[75] So I participate in praising with the angels. And the priest says in the Liturgy according to St. Gregory, "[You have] given to the earthly the praising of the seraphim."[76] The praise of the seraphim revolves around the word "holy."

And we are reminded that without holiness, no one will see the Lord, as St. Paul the Apostle said in the epistle to the Hebrews, "Pursue peace with all people,

---

72 The Divine Liturgy of St. Gregory – The Anaphora.
73 The Divine Liturgy of St. Basil – The Liturgy of the Faithful.
74 The Raising of Morning Incense – The Gloria.
75 The Divine Liturgy of St. Basil – The Liturgy of the Faithful.
76 The Divine Liturgy of St. Gregory – The Anaphora.

and holiness, without which no one will see the Lord."[77] And without holiness, we do not participate in the sacrifice of the Liturgy, because the sacrifice of the Liturgy is a gathering of the sanctified of the people and angels together in the presence of the Lord. This makes the priest, at the end of the Liturgy, say, "The Holies for the holy." So every time we say the praise of the angels—"Holy, holy, holy, Lord of hosts,"—the person at this time ought to ask for holiness, with tears and contrition, and struggle for its sake. We chant their praise, and the angels repeat our prayers in exchange.

As we have said about intercessions, we pray for the saints, and the saints pray for us; we participate in the praise with the angels, and so we praise with the angels, and the angels participate with us. In the Liturgy according to St. Gregory, we say, "[He] who has established the rising of the choir of the incorporeal among men."[78] The incorporeal are the angels, which means that the Lord established their rising among us. In the Divine Liturgy, the angels are standing among men. And in the Litany for the Oblations, the priest says, "Receive them upon Your holy, rational altar in heaven as a sweet savor of incense before Your greatness in the heavens, through the service of Your holy angels and archangels."

And concerning their presence in the Liturgy, when the priest takes water at the end of the Liturgy and raises it, he says, "O angel of this sacrifice, flying up to the

---

[77] Hebrews 12:14.
[78] The Divine Liturgy of St. Gregory – The Anaphora.

In the Divine Liturgy, I Understand...

heights with this hymn, remember us before the Lord." Similarly, we read in the Book of Acts that there was an angel who took the prayers of Cornelius and lifted them up to heaven.[79] We sing their praises, and they sing ours. In The Divine Liturgy of St. Gregory, he says, "They send up the hymn of victory and salvation which is ours, with a voice full of glory."[80] They sing our hymn with a voice full of glory. Where do we get this from, that they sing our hymn? In the Book of Revelation, the heavenly hosts, the four living creatures and the twenty-four priests, say, "You are worthy to take the scroll, and to open its seals; for You were slain, and have redeemed us to God by Your blood out of every tribe and tongue and people and nation, and have made us kings and priests to our God."[81] Was the Lord slain for the sake of the angels, and redeemed them by His blood? No; rather, they were united with us: "[He] who has established the rising of the choir of the incorporeal among men."[82] As we sing their hymn, "Holy, holy, holy," so do they also sing our hymn, praying with our words, "You were slain, and have redeemed us to God by Your blood out of every tribe and tongue and people and nation, and have made us kings and priests to our God." Here the angels sing our hymn, and take our prayers and pray them as though they were us, because "He made the two into one, that is the heaven and the earth."

---

79 See Acts 10.
80 The Divine Liturgy of St. Gregory – The Anaphora.
81 Revelation 5:9–10.
82 The Divine Liturgy of St. Gregory – The Anaphora.

Also concerning the praising of the angels, the priest says in the Liturgy that they praise with one voice,[83] meaning that they all participate in praising. So, let us learn that we all ought to participate in praising, and not only the one person who is standing at the microphone. We should all participate and should not sing alone, but with one voice. Also, we should not sing lazily, for the priest says, "They cry out, saying."[84] So we should praise neither lazily nor conceitedly, but humbly, with an angelic voice, with fear and reverence. As the angels stand with reverence, so should we stand before God, praising with the angels, humbly as the tax collector stood with his head bowed, seeking mercy.

So does the priest say in the Fraction, "And even as You have cleansed the lips of Your servant Isaiah the prophet, as one of the seraphim took an ember with the tongs from the altar, cast it into his mouth, and said to him, 'Behold, this has touched your lips, it shall take away your iniquities and cleanse all your sins.' Likewise we too, the weak sinners, Your pitiable servants, graciously cleanse our souls, our bodies, our lips, and our hearts; and give us this true Ember that is life-giving to soul, body, and spirit, which is the holy Body and the precious Blood of Your Christ."[85] So we say to Him: Lord, as the seraphim took an ember from the altar and placed it into Isaiah's mouth, saying to him, "When this touches your lips, your iniquities are taken away and all

---

83 See ibid.
84 Ibid.
85 Standard Cyrillian Fraction.

your sins are cleansed," so we have eaten of this same Ember. And this Ember is the body and blood which we partake of in the Divine Liturgy. "Cleanse our souls, our bodies, our lips, and our hearts."

Therefore, the words of the Divine Liturgy are not mere entreaties like any ordinary prayer, but are tools and instruments in the hand of the Holy Spirit to sanctify the oblations and change them to the body of the Lord and His blood. And all the congregation stands still, awaiting these awesome moments, the moments of the descent of the Holy Spirit upon the bread and wine to change them to the body of the Lord and His blood. The deacon says, "Worship God in fear and trembling," and all the congregation worships and says, "We praise You, we bless You, we serve You, we worship You." They are not waiting for an angel to move the water, as in the pool of Bethesda, but are waiting for the Holy Spirit to perform the miracle of miracles, changing the bread and wine to the body of the Lord and His blood. And before the Altar is a great multitude of sick people, lame and paralyzed, so that He may spread healing for the sicknesses of sin: "Given for us for salvation, remission of sins, and eternal life to those who partake of Him."[86]

In the Divine Liturgy, we are not standing before the pool of Bethesda, but before the Altar of the Lord of hosts, before the "holy, rational altar in heaven."[87]

---

86 The Divine Liturgy of St. Basil – The Confession.
87 The Divine Liturgy of St. Basil – The Three Long Litanies.

We are not waiting for an angel to move the water, but we are waiting for the Creator of the angels to heal us from the lust of the flesh, as He healed Mary Magdalene; from the sickness of hastiness and denial, as He healed Peter; from the sickness of fear, as He healed Nicodemus who came at night to Christ; from the sickness of the love of money, as He healed Zacchaeus; and from the sickness of murder and stealing, as He healed the right hand thief. For this reason, in the litany for the sick, the priest prays, saying, "The spirit of sicknesses, chase away.... Those who are afflicted by unclean spirits, set them all free. Those who are in prisons or dungeons, those who are in exile or captivity, or those who are held in bitter bondage, O Lord, set them all free and have mercy upon them. For You are He who loosens the bound and uplifts the fallen.... O You, the true physician of our souls and bodies, the Bishop of all flesh, visit us with Your salvation."

St. John Chrysostom says that the Church is not a hotel for saints but a hospital for sinners. God does not seek to recompense them in the Divine Liturgy, but seeks to forgive them and heal them. For in the Divine Liturgy, I come as a sinner, not so that I may be judged and punished, but I come as a sinner to be justified and to be healed of the sicknesses of sin, and for my sin to be forgiven: "Given for us for salvation, remission of sins, and eternal life to those who partake of Him."[88]

---

88 The Divine Liturgy of St. Basil – The Confession.

The Divine Liturgy: The Journey of My Life with Christ

The Divine Liturgy is the journey of my life with the Lord Christ, from His Incarnation to His Ascension to heaven. For the Divine Liturgy makes the incarnation present with us always, regardless of the chronological order of events, because we go out of the boundaries of time and place. The body of the Lord and His blood are present with us upon the Altar: "Behold Immanuel our God, the Lamb of God who takes away the sin of the whole world, is with us today on this table."[89] As we say in Midnight Praises: "For the One without flesh was incarnate… and the eternal One became temporal."[90]

When we do a commemoration, we usually commemorate something that happened in the past. We celebrate, for example, our 20th wedding anniversary, or our son's fifteenth birthday, and so on. In the Divine Liturgy, however, we say, "Therefore, as we also commemorate His holy Passion, His Resurrection from the dead, His Ascension into the heavens, His Sitting at Your right hand, O Father."[91] So far, there is no issue, since all of these happened in the past—the Passion, Resurrection, Ascension, and Sitting at the right hand of the Father. Then the priest continues, saying, "and His Second Coming

---

89 The Fraction for the Feasts of the Virgin and Angels.
90 The Wednesday Theotokia Part 7.
91 The Divine Liturgy of St. Basil – The Institution Narrative.

from the heavens, awesome and full of glory." How am I living the Second Coming of Christ in the Divine Liturgy? Because, in the Liturgy, we are outside the boundaries of time and place. In the Second Coming, Christ will come so that He will be present with us, and He is right now present with us—"Behold Immanuel our God, the Lamb of God who takes away the sin of the whole world, is with us today on this table."[92] Therefore, in the Divine Liturgy, I celebrate the coming of the Lord; I live the Second Coming of the Lord, "His Second Coming from the heavens, awesome and full of glory." In the Divine Liturgy, therefore, I live the mystery of the Incarnation of Christ.

In the Divine Liturgy, He said, "Take, eat; this is My body which is broken for you"[93] So I partake with the Lord of His sufferings for the sake of the world, because I eat of the sacrificed body of Christ. I partake with Him of His sufferings for the sake of the world and the sinners. I keep watch with Him in Gethsemane, as He was passing through sorrow even to death.[94] I partake of His body and drink of His blood, and participate with Him in the cup of my brethren, the sons of men. And so, my brethren's sins become my sins, and I offer repentance, because I and they are one. I am a sinner, and they are my brethren in the body of the Lord.

---

92 The Fraction for the Feasts of the Virgin and Angels.
93 1 Corinthians 11:24.
94 See Matthew 26:38.

In the Divine Liturgy, as I said, as Christ was sacrificed, I sacrifice: "I offer You, O my Master, the symbols of my freedom."[95] So I am led to the slaughter with Him, as a lamb that opens not its mouth.[96] I partake of His body and blood, so I receive the power of slaughtering my will, and "I write my works according to Your sayings."[97] I live the Incarnation and the sufferings, and I am led to the slaughter.

In the Divine Liturgy, I receive the power of the death upon the cross, because I partake of His crucified body, and I testify to His power, saying, "I have been crucified with Christ."[98] "Those who are Christ's have crucified the flesh with its passions and desires."[99] And I testify to the power of the cross of Christ, "by whom the world has been crucified to me, and I to the world."[100] In the Divine Liturgy, I see Christ pierced, and I see His precious blood shed and present in the chalice upon the Altar. And so I drink of His precious blood, the holy blood that washes away my sins, cleanses me of my iniquities, and heals me of my spiritual and bodily sicknesses.

In the Divine Liturgy, I go to the tomb and find it empty, and so I preach the power of the Resurrection: "For every time you eat of this bread and drink

---

95 The Divine Liturgy of St. Gregory – The Institution Narrative.
96 See Isaiah 53:7.
97 Ibid.
98 Galatians 2:20.
99 Galatians 5:24.
100 Galatians 6:14.

of this cup, you proclaim My Death, confess My Resurrection,"[101] because I eat of His living body that is resurrected from the dead, so the life of Christ may be manifested in my mortal body.[102] In the Divine Liturgy, I go with the disciples to the Mount of Olives, and I behold Christ ascending on the clouds, and so I eat of His body and live in this sight, being drawn with my heart to heaven until He comes and takes me with Him on the clouds. In the Divine Liturgy, I live the Second Coming of the Lord, and I say to Him, "Amen. Even so, come, Lord Jesus!"[103]

Thus, the Divine Liturgy is truly the greatest work humankind does on earth. Poor is the person who does not attend the Liturgy. Poor is the person who comes late to the Liturgy. Poor is the person who stands in the Liturgy while their mind is distracted. Poor is the person who is preoccupied with a million things during the Liturgy, who is unable to delight in all the meanings that are in the Divine Liturgy. For this reason, Pope Kyrillos loved the Altar and the Divine Liturgy; for this reason, he prayed the Divine Liturgy every day, for how could he enjoy all these blessings and all these gifts, without the Liturgy? The Divine Liturgy for him was his life; therefore, even at the peak of his sickness, he used to pray the Divine Liturgy, not refraining from attending the Liturgy regardless of the circumstances.

---

101 The Divine Liturgy of St. Basil – The Institution Narrative.
102 See 2 Corinthians 2:10.
103 Revelation 22:20.

Appendix

Four Fellowship-related Words

First, I would like to define the four words that are related to the word "fellowship" or the word "*koinonia*" (Gr.) and to explain these four terms from a Christian perspective. Then we will see together how the ultimate fellowship is in the Divine Liturgy, and the word "liturgy" means the work of the people. *Laos* (Gr.) means people, and *urgos* (Gr.) means work, so people working together or praying together or worshipping together.

1. Relationship

"Relationship" is the first word that is related to fellowship. When we hear the word fellowship, this means that there is a relationship.

In the New Testament, what is shared in common is first shared because of the common relationship we all have in Christ. What made the people, during the time of the apostles, sell their possessions and bring the proceeds, and put them at the feet of the apostles? It is not like communism; it is totally different, because all of us are one in Christ. This is why we need to share everything. Therefore, this important relationship with one another in Christ is the foundation of fellowship. Earthly fellowship or secular fellowship is founded upon common interests or human nature, or physical ties, like in a family, but this is not the New Testament fellowship.

In First Corinthians, St. Paul says, "God is faithful, by whom you were called into the fellowship of His Son, Jesus Christ our Lord."[104] God called us to have fellowship in His Son Jesus Christ, because, as I have previously said, in baptism I am not an individual anymore but a member of the body of Christ. In the secular world, fellowship is just an activity, but in Christianity, fellowship is a relationship more than just an activity. Therefore, in any activity that is based on this relationship, we are bonded together, we are united together in the body of Christ. The people in the early Church did not devote themselves to activities like attending spiritual meetings or going together to church, but they were committed, and they devoted themselves to a relationship, and this relationship produced all these different activities. Think about it like marriage. Marriage is not about common activities; marriage is about a relationship and a commitment to one another, and then activity is

---
104 1 Corinthians 1:9.

the outcome of this relationship. This is the Christian fellowship: it is not about activities together. It is not just that we have a meeting together; it is a relationship together in Christ.

2. Partnership

The second word is partnership. In Christian fellowship, there is a partnership. We say in the Divine Liturgy about the Pope and the bishop, "And his partner in the apostolic liturgy." Some people think that this is a mistranslation, that we should say, "And his partner in the apostolic service or apostolic ministry." What do you mean by "partner in the liturgy"? If I am not a partner in the liturgy, then I am not a partner in the ministry. If I cannot be a partner in the liturgy, how can we partake of the same body together and be partners in ministry? So our partnership is mainly in the liturgy; we eat of the same bread and drink of the same cup. If we are not in Communion, then we are not partners.

In the Holy Scriptures, the word partner is used to refer to both the secular and the Christian fellowship. In his gospel, St. Luke spoke about how James and John were partners with Peter and Andrew, as fishermen;[105] this is a secular partnership. But it is also used in a spiritual sense, like what St. Paul said, "If anyone inquires about Titus, he is my partner and fellow worker concerning you. Or if our brethren are inquired

---
105 See Luke 5:7, 10.

about, they are messengers of the churches, the glory of Christ."[106] So he used the word partner here.

So, what is the difference between the words "relationship" and "partnership"? Relationship describes the believers as a community, but partnership describes the believers as the principals of an enterprise. We are partners as in a business partnership; there is an objective, and each one provides toward this goal or toward this objective, and at the end, all partners profit from this objective or this goal. In the same way, in spiritual partnership, there is an objective for us; what is this objective? To glorify Christ, as St. Paul said. Whatever we do, whether we eat or drink or do anything else, we do it all for the glory of God. So we are partners together to glorify God, and we are united together in this community to glorify God.

In the Divine Liturgy, we start by glorifying God, and we conclude by glorifying God. The first thing we say in the Divine Liturgy, "Glory and honor, and honor and glory to the All-Holy Trinity, the Father and the Son and the Holy Spirit."[107] It is as if the priest, at the beginning of the Divine Liturgy, brings the goal to our attention: We assembled together today to glorify God. And after he makes the three signings—"Blessed be God the Father, the Pantocrator... Blessed be His only-begotten Son, Jesus Christ our Lord... Blessed be the Holy Spirit, the Paraclete,"[108]—and the

---
106 2 Corinthians 8:23.
107 The Offering of the Lamb.
108 Ibid.

congregation chants and sings, saying, "Glory to the Father and the Son and the Holy Spirit, now and ever and unto the ages of the ages. Amen. Alleluia."

Then at the end of the Divine Liturgy, in the last passage, which is before the Introduction to the Fraction—because the Introduction to the Fraction, the Fraction, and the Confession are considered the beginning of Communion—in this last passage the priest says, "Lead us throughout the way into Your kingdom, that as in this, so also in all things, Your great and holy name may be glorified, blessed, and exalted in everything honored and blessed, with Jesus Christ, Your beloved Son, and the Holy Spirit." So in the Divine Liturgy, the priest, by saying "You are glorified, blessed and exalted, with Your beloved Son and the Holy Spirit," is concluding by glorifying the Holy Trinity.

Also, during Communion, the whole congregation says, "Praise God in all His saints." Therefore, when we commune together, when we assemble in the Divine Liturgy, we are partners in the Divine Liturgy to praise God, which is the goal in front of us. We are here to praise God, and through praising God, we become one when we partake of His body and His blood, and through this oneness, our fellowship with one another is actualized. I told you that in business, there is a profit. What is the profit from this partnership in the Liturgy? "Given for us for salvation, remission of sins, and eternal life to those who partake of Him."[109]

---

109 The Divine Liturgy of St. Basil – The Confession.

This partnership begins on earth, but it will continue with us in heaven, and this partnership gives us the inheritance of the kingdom of God. A partner owns something. If you are a business partner, you own something in this business. In the epistle to the Romans, St. Paul spoke about our partnership and said, "The Spirit Himself bears witness with our spirit that we are children of God, and if children, then heirs—heirs of God and joint heirs with Christ, if indeed we suffer with Him, that we may also be glorified together."[110] "Heirs"—so we will have inheritance. We will inherit the kingdom of God. Inheritance means our own.

We need to again understand that the word fellowship, the Christian fellowship, means relationship as a community. We are related to one another. Also, we are partners with Christ. That is, a community of people bound together by our common life and the blessing that we share through our relationship with the Holy Trinity. Partnership describes how we are related to one another in this relationship.

3. Companionship

The third word under the word fellowship is companionship. Companionship happens through communication. You cannot have a companion with whom you never communicate. Therefore, communication is a very important point and is

---
110 Romans 8:16–17.

the key ingredient in any companionship. In any fellowship, we need to have communication with God and communications with one another, that is to say, vertical communication and horizontal communications. Vertical communication is with God and with the cloud of witnesses in paradise, while horizontal communications are with one another in the body of Christ. This includes that we assemble as one body in church, and that we also assemble in small groups or even meet together one on one.

Let us take biblical examples of each one. Regarding assembling together as a whole body, we read in the Book of Acts, "And they continued steadfastly in the apostles' doctrine and fellowship, in the breaking of bread, and in prayers."[111] The whole community assembled together listening to the teaching of the apostles, in fellowship, in prayers, in the breaking of bread that is Communion. Regarding small groups, St. Paul said to Timothy, "And the things that you have heard from me among many witnesses, commit these to faithful men who will be able to teach others also."[112] This is similar to the meetings we have: meeting with the servants, meeting with the deacons, meeting with the service coordinators. So St. Paul is saying to Timothy, "What you heard from me among many witnesses, commit these to faithful men who will be able to teach others also." Regarding one on one, St. Paul said, "Therefore comfort each other and

---

111 Acts 2:42.
112 2 Timothy 2:2.

edify one another, just as you also are doing."[113] "Edify one another" is like the visitations that Sunday school servants do, going and visiting one person and talking to them one on one. All these are different styles of communications on the horizontal level.

Building one another is also an example of horizontal communications. As we read in the epistle to the Romans, St. Paul said to them, "For I long to see you, that I may impart to you some spiritual gift, so that you may be established—that is, that I may be encouraged together with you by the mutual faith both of you and me."[114] It is like when His Holiness the Pope pays us a visit, or one of the bishops or priests. So this is how we built one another as St. Paul told them: "I long to see you that I may impart to you some spiritual gift so that you may be established. Not only will you be established by the spiritual gift that I will impart to you, but I may be encouraged together with you by the mutual faith of you and me."

Another example of horizontal communications is participating together in worship. Concerning our fellowship with one another, St. Paul said, "The cup of blessing which we bless, is it not the communion of the blood of Christ? The bread which we break, is it not the communion of the body of Christ? For we, though many, are one bread and one body; for we all partake of that one bread."[115] So this is another

---
113 1 Thessalonians 5:11.
114 Romans 1:11–12.
115 1 Corinthians 10:16–17.

way of communication when we participate together in singing and praising the Lord during the Divine Liturgy.

Another example of horizontal communications is when we carry the burdens of one another, like what St. Paul mentioned, saying, "Bear one another's burdens, and so fulfill the law of Christ."[116] Therefore, we need to carry the burdens of one another and to help one another. So, this is a different type of fellowship. As I have said that companionship—communication—is a very essential element in fellowship. If we do not communicate with one another, then we do not have a true Christian fellowship.

We mentioned three words so far. Fellowship means relationship. We are related to one another; we are members of one another in one body. Fellowship means partnership. Not only are we related, but we are also partners together and partners with Christ. As partners, we will inherit the kingdom of God. We are partners together with one goal, that is, to glorify God in our lives. And we will also obtain a profit: "Given for us for salvation, remission of sins, and eternal life to those who partake of Him."[117] And the third word is companionship or communication with one another. Communication happens at the same time on the vertical level between us and God and the horizontal level. I mentioned different examples of the horizontal

---

116 Galatians 6:2.
117 The Divine Liturgy of St. Basil – The Confession.

level, such as assembling as one body, assembling in a small group, meeting together one on one, building one another, participating in worship, and carrying the burdens of one another.

4. Stewardship

The last word under fellowship is stewardship. A steward is the one who manages the property of another. A steward is not the owner, but he is a manager. All of us are stewards; therefore, as stewards, we must recognize that we all belong to the Lord, that God has entrusted us with certain gifts, and that these gifts are for us to use to serve one another, and this will strengthen our fellowship.

They say that gifts are like a toolbox, not a jewelry box. Why is that? We usually use jewelry to adorn ourselves with, but tools we use to serve one another with. God gave us gifts not for our own glory, not to adorn ourselves with these gifts, but God gave us gifts as stewards to serve others with them. As we read in the first epistle of St. Peter, it says, "As each one has received a gift, minister it to one another, as good stewards of the manifold grace of God."[118] We cannot be in fellowship without using our stewardship, our gifts, to serve one another. You need to know what your gifts are and how to use these gifts to serve others. In the epistle to the Romans, St. Paul said:

---

118 1 Peter 4:10.

So we, being many, are one body in Christ, and individually members of one another. Having then gifts differing according to the grace that is given to us, let us use them: if prophecy, let us prophesy in proportion to our faith; or ministry, let us use it in our ministering; he who teaches, in teaching; he who exhorts, in exhortation; he who gives, with liberality; he who leads, with diligence; he who shows mercy, with cheerfulness.[119]

So, who will decide which gift you will receive and how many gifts you will receive? It is God, as St. Paul said. St. Paul is saying that if we are members in one body, and God gives us these gifts, let us use these gifts as good and faithful stewards to serve one another. I should not keep the gift for myself, nor should I hide the gift or bury it. The steward who took the one talent from the master and buried it, the master said to him, "You wicked and lazy servant."[120] You need to know what your gifts are and how to use them to serve your brothers and sisters in Christ; otherwise, we are not in fellowship.

Concluding Remarks

Therefore, we need to understand these four words related to fellowship. I am not in fellowship if I do

---

119 Romans 12:5–8.
120 Matthew 25:26.

not feel that I am related to all of you. I am related to all of you because I am a part of the body of Christ, and you are part of the same body. We are related and are connected with one another; we eat of the same bread and drink of the same cup. Also, we are partners together; not only are we related, but we are also partners together, partners in praising God and in glorifying Him. All of us together will reflect the attributes of God, the light of Christ, the light of God to the whole world. And if we are in fellowship, we need to communicate. Communication with God is the vertical level, and communications with one another are the horizontal level. And the last point, as a steward, each one has received a gift from God, so let us serve one another with these gifts as good and faithful stewards.

Then, as I said, the application or the ultimate fellowship is in the Divine Liturgy. In the Divine Liturgy, these four elements are fulfilled. All of us stand together, and we greet one another with a holy kiss, meaning that we are related to each other, that we are members in the body of Christ. We are partners in worshiping and praising God. And we communicate with God and communicate with one another during the Divine Liturgy. Communication with God is through our prayers, and with one another is, for example, when we greet one another with a holy kiss or when we pray for each other during the Divine Liturgy. The deacon says several times, "Pray for the peace of the Church," "Pray for our Patriarch," "Pray for the clergy," "Pray for the salvation of this holy place." These prayers are a type of communication with one another. Also, as stewards, we use our stewardship in glorifying God: those who chant, those who read, those who preach, those who teach.

So the Divine Liturgy is indeed the ultimate fellowship. Besides, the Divine Liturgy is a fellowship in the suffering of the Lord and His resurrection, as the Lord said, and the priest quotes Him in the Divine Liturgy, saying, "For every time you eat of this bread and drink of this cup, you proclaim My Death, confess My Resurrection, and remember Me till I come."[121] What does this mean? Why is it that every time you eat of this bread and drink of this cup in the Divine Liturgy, you can remember the passion of the Lord and His death at any moment, and can remember His resurrection at any moment? Why in the Divine Liturgy? Because in the Divine Liturgy we live it. We do not just remember it in our minds, but we live it. How do we live it? When we partake of the broken Body and drink of the Blood that was shed for our sake, we participate in the passions of the Lord. And that is why the Lord said, "Take, eat; this is My body which is broken for you,"[122] and, "This cup is the new covenant in My blood, which is shed for you."[123]

In the Divine Liturgy, the Body that is on the Altar is the crucified Body, which is why the bread is

---

121 The Divine Liturgy of St. Basil – The Institution Narrative.
122 1 Corinthians 11:24.
123 Luke 22:20.

made with yeast. Yeast is a symbol of sin. Jesus Christ lived His life without sin, but on the cross He carried our sins. That is why this sacrifice is the sacrifice of the crucified Lord, and that is why the Body is given separately from His blood, because this body was broken. That is why the Lord said, "Take, eat; this is My body.... Drink from it, all of you. For this is My blood."[124] Even in the epistle to the Corinthians, St. Paul said:

> For I received from the Lord that which I also delivered to you: that the Lord Jesus on the same night in which He was betrayed took bread; and when He had given thanks, He broke it and said, "Take, eat; this is My body which is broken for you; do this in remembrance of Me." In the same manner He also took the cup after supper, saying, "This cup is the new covenant in My blood. This do, as often as you drink it, in remembrance of Me."[125]

Therefore, there were two separate actions: Body and Blood, because that is the crucified Lord. So when we partake of His body and partake of His blood, it is a participation, a fellowship in the passion of the Lord.

Also, this Body is a life-giving flesh. So we who are under the sentence of death because of our sins, when

---

124 Matthew 26:26–28.
125 1 Corinthians 11:23–25.

we eat of His body, He gives us life. At the end of the Divine Liturgy, the priest says, "I believe, I believe, I believe and confess to the last breath that this is the life-giving Flesh.... given for us for salvation, remission of sins, and eternal life to those who partake of Him."[126] That is why every time we partake of His body and His blood, we live His passion and His resurrection, both His death and His resurrection, because it is the crucified Body and the same Body rose from the dead, so this is why the Lord said that every time you eat of My body and drink of My blood, you remember My death and confess My resurrection. So, it is a real fellowship in the passion of the Lord and His resurrection. And if you notice, when the priest breaks the Body, he breaks the Body into thirteen pieces. Why thirteen pieces? Jesus Christ, the head, and the twelve pieces are like the twelve apostles or the twelve tribes of Israel, symbolizing the Church. So, in Communion, the Eucharist makes the body one with the head. We are the body, and He is the head of the body. So, when we partake of His body and drink of His blood, we are one. This is fellowship, our fellowship with the Father and His Son Jesus Christ. That is why the Eucharist is sometimes called "Communion,"[127] and I told you the word "partner" or "partake" is an important description of the fellowship; so we partake. Therefore, the ultimate expression of fellowship is in the Divine Liturgy.

---

126 The Divine Liturgy of St. Basil – The Confession.

127 The Arabic word for Communion could also mean partaking.

www.ingramcontent.com/pod-product-compliance
Lightning Source LLC
Chambersburg PA
CBHW031416040426
42444CB00005B/587